PRESENTED TO

_____

FROM

_____

DATE

_____

A POCKET GUIDE
TO PRAYER

Steve Harper

UPPER
ROOM BOOKS®
NASHVILLE

A POCKET GUIDE TO PRAYER

Copyright © 2010 by Steve Harper

No part of this book may be reproduced in any manner whatsoever without written permission of the publisher except in brief quotations embodied in critical articles or reviews. For information, write Upper Room Books, 1908 Grand Avenue, Nashville, TN 37212.

The Upper Room Web site: www.upperroom.org

UPPER ROOM®, UPPER ROOM BOOKS®, and design logos are trademarks owned by The Upper Room®, a ministry of GBOD®, Nashville, Tennessee. All rights reserved.

Page 141 constitutes an extension of this copyright page.

Cover design: Bruce Gore / Gore Studio
First printing: 2010

LIBRARY OF CONGRESS CATALOGING-IN-PUBLICATION DATA

Harper, Steve, 1947–
  A pocket guide to prayer / written & compiled by Steve Harper.
    p. cm.
  ISBN 978-0-8358-1042-5
  1. Prayer—Christianity. I. Title.
  BV210.3.H364 2011
  248.3'2—dc22

                                                2010036368

Printed in the United States of America

Contents

PREFACE

NOTHING SUBSTITUTES FOR TIME alone with God. Whatever we call it—the daily office, quiet time, devotions—it is the work of the heart, from whence everything else springs in the life of Christian holiness. Throughout the history of Christian spirituality, manuals of devotion have been produced to assist disciples in their formation. This prayer book now comes to join those in both purpose and content.

In our day and time we are witnessing a new emergence of the Spirit all over the earth and, along with it, a new commitment to the practice of the means of grace and the keeping of other spiritual disciplines. Living liturgy and accompanying forms of prayer are as necessary now as ever to sustain the life of faith. This little book will help establish you in classic formational elements that Christians today are practicing with renewed devotion.

I was moved to produce this pocket guide to prayer because of my use of an earlier, similar volume compiled by Ralph Cushman. *A Pocket Prayer Book* remains a classic work and serves as a valuable resource in my formation.

I pray that this current volume will be used by God for purposes similar to those achieved in Cushman's work—to cultivate the life of God in the human soul and to sustain the holy habits of prayer and devotion. To that end, I offer you the prayer that Ralph Cushman wrote to introduce his little volume.

—STEVE HARPER

Set us afire, Lord,
Stir us, we pray!
While the world perishes
We go our way,
Purposeless, passionless,
Day after day.
Set us afire, Lord,
Stir us, we pray!

—RALPH S. CUSHMAN

Holy Time

GOD GIVES EACH of us the same amount of time. The difference comes in how we understand and make use of the gift. Time must be organized and managed, but it must also be consecrated. Spiritual formation integrates these activities, with the result that time becomes holy. Sacred time provides the space for the work of the heart and the actions of the hands.

From Old Testament times until now, literary sources indicate that men and women of faith arranged their days and punctuated their time with particular moments of personal and corporate worship. While specific patterns and practices vary widely, spiritually minded persons acknowledge the essential nature of stated devotional acts throughout the day to spiritual well-being. This prayer book honors one historic pattern comprised of five daily times of prayer; yet it leaves room for adaptation and expansion of the fundamental cycle.

Equally visible in the history of Christian spirituality is the importance of singing. The book of Psalms served as Israel's songbook. Jesus and his disciples sang (Matt. 26:30), as did the early Christians (Eph. 5:19). The devotional life has always included what John Wesley called "hymns and other prayers." This daily order of devotion includes a place for praying the psalms and singing.

The aim of it all is to "pray without ceasing" (1 Thess. 5:17). God does not call us to have a devotional *time* but to live a devotional *life*. Any specific time of prayer is meant to produce a greater awareness that all time is God's time, that every moment is a God-moment.

Only then will we experience living faith: holiness of heart and life.

> *Read and pray daily.*
> *It is for your life;*
> *There is no other way:*
> *Else you will be a trifler*
> *All your days.*

—JOHN WESLEY

1.

Prayer upon Awakening

Prayer upon awakening has always been part of Christian devotion. We center our early attention on God. We thank God for giving us another day to live, and we ask the Holy Spirit to guide us in the living of it. We recommit ourselves to be instruments of God's peace. Prayers upon awakening ignite our gratitude and focus our resolve.

The prayers in this section and those that follow it are intentionally written in first-person language. The assumption is that you will normally use this book in your personal devotions. But it is important to remember that none of us ever prays alone. We always pray in community with all others who are praying. At times, you may wish to change the "I" language to "We" language as a recognition of this great truth. Nothing in this prayer book is meant to advocate or encourage individualism or separateness.

Upon awakening in the morning, say:

Glory be to the Father, and to the Son, and to the Holy Spirit. Amen.

Dear God, I rise from my bed of sleep, to adore your holy name, to live for you this day, to work with you in the building of your kingdom, and to find in you eternal life. In the name of the Father, Son, and Holy Spirit. Amen.

Renew your will to worship and serve God in this new day:

Sunday: I rise to love you with all my heart, soul, mind, and strength.

Monday: I resolve to love my neighbor as myself.

Tuesday: I desire to walk humbly with you.

Wednesday: I utterly renounce everything that enlarges my ego and reduces my dependence upon you.

Thursday: I seek to live so close to you today that your glory shall be my only aim and your will shall be my only desire.

Friday: I invite you to reveal all my offenses and to forgive all my sins.

Saturday: I want to prepare to worship you aright tomorrow.

Having thus sought the presence of God and resolved to live for God this day, now affirm your faith:

I believe in God, the Father Almighty,
    maker of heaven and earth;

And in Jesus Christ, his only Son our Lord:
who was conceived by the Holy Spirit,
    born of the Virgin Mary,
    suffered under Pontius Pilate,
    was crucified, dead, and buried;
the third day he rose from the dead;
he ascended into heaven,
    and sitteth at the right hand of God
    the Father Almighty;
from thence he shall come to judge the
    quick and the dead.

I believe in the Holy Spirit,
    the holy catholic church,
    the communion of saints,
    the forgiveness of sins,
    the resurrection of the body,
    and the life everlasting. Amen.

Conclude this time of awakening by praying:

Come, Holy Spirit. Be my guide and
the guardian of all my ways. Fill me
anew with yourself that I may manifest
your fruit: love, joy, peace, patience,
kindness, goodness, faithfulness, gentleness, and self-control. Amen.

*Now turn to those activities that help you prepare
yourself for the new day, using those activities as further preparation for your time of morning prayer.*

2.

Morning Prayer

Morning prayer is a time of recognition that God, who never slumbers or sleeps, has been at work while we have been at rest. Morning prayer is not the beginning of the day; it is our first response to grace in the day. It is an act of anticipation—reorienting ourselves to God, affirming our faith, and renewing our intention to live for God in this new day.

In both ancient and modern traditions, morning prayer has often been a communal act of worship. If you are able, use this section with others, modifying the first-person language as you like. But you may be using this section by yourself. As you do so, remind yourself once again that you never pray alone. God is right where you are and, as you pray, you are connecting with others all over the world who are also praying.

When you are ready, find your accustomed devotional place or another suitable location for this time of prayer, renewing your covenant with God.

Sunday: O LORD, in the morning you hear my voice; in the morning I plead my case to you, and watch (Ps. 5:3).

Monday: I will give thanks to the LORD with my whole heart; I will tell of all your wonderful deeds (Ps. 9:1).

Tuesday: I say to the LORD, "You are my Lord; I have no good apart from you" (Ps. 16:2).

Wednesday: I call upon the LORD, who is worthy to be praised, so I shall be saved from my enemies (Ps. 18:3).

Thursday: My heart is steadfast, O God, my heart is steadfast. I will sing and make melody (Ps. 57:7).

Friday: For God alone my soul waits in silence; from him comes my salvation (Ps. 62:1).

Saturday: O God, you are my God, I seek you, my soul thirsts for you (Ps. 63:1).

The Invitatory

O God, come to our assistance.
O God, hurry to save us.
O God, hasten to help us.

Glory be to the Father, and to the Son, and to the Holy Spirit; as it was in the beginning, is now, and will be forever. Amen.

Hymn of the Day

Sing the appointed hymn for the day of the month (pages 35–98).

Psalm of the Day

Pray the appointed psalm, using the schedule on page 34.

Reading of the Morning

Follow a daily lectionary or another devotional plan of your choice.

Meditation

In silence, reflect upon what you have read and "take a word" (idea) that you want to use for further thought and guidance in the day.

Prayer of the Day

Pray the appointed prayer for the day of the month (pages 35–98).

The Lord's Prayer (Matt. 6:9-13)

Our Father in heaven,
> hallowed be your name.
> Your kingdom come.

Your will be done,
    on earth as it is in heaven.
Give us this day our daily bread.
And forgive us our debts,
    as we also have forgiven our debtors.
And do not bring us to the time of trial,
    but rescue us from the evil one.

Benediction

May the God of hope fill us with all joy and peace in believing, so that we may abound in hope by the power of the Holy Spirit. Amen. (based on Rom. 15:13)

3.

NOONTIME PRAYER

NOONTIME PRAYER relates to the hours that Christ hung on the cross for our redemption. Some traditions add prayers at 9:00 AM and 3:00 PM to further emphasize his death, remembering the other two hours when he spoke from the cross.

Coming at midday, noontime prayer offers an occasion to express our gratitude for Christ's redemption and to recommit ourselves to being his witness to that redemption for the rest of the day. Noontime prayer gives us the occasion to pray for those things that have happened in the morning, as well as to seek grace to face the things that are yet to come. In the early church, Wednesdays and Fridays were set aside as days to fast during the noon hour.

In all cases, noontime prayer provides an occasion to further hallow the life God has given us.

As you prepare to go to lunch or to practice a noonday fast, pray:

O God, come to my assistance.
O God, save me now.
O God, help me quickly.

Glory be to the Father, and to the Son, and to the Holy Spirit; as it was in the beginning, is now, and will be forever. Amen.

Then pray the following prayer or one like it:

Gracious God, at this hour of the day, your Son suffered on the cross for my redemption. I accept anew the gift of his salvation and offer myself as a witness to that salvation.

In the generous portion of the day that remains, give me grace to be attentive to the needs of those around me that I may continue to offer myself to you as a living sacrifice. Direct me as you like; use me as you will. I ask no more than this. Amen.

Pray for particular needs that have arisen thus far today and for those things you know will come up before the end of the day.

Pray The Lord's Prayer

Then say:

Let the words of my mouth, and the meditation of my heart, be acceptable in thy sight, O LORD, my strength, and my redeemer (Ps. 19:14, KJV).

If you are eating a meal, say grace over it. If you are fasting, ask that the time you would normally spend eating may be spent in a way that honors God and grows your soul.

4.

EVENING PRAYER

THE LIFE OF PRAYER includes review as well as anticipation. Evening prayer provides the opportunity to look back upon the day you have lived, rejoice in those things you have done well, repent of any sins you've committed, and resolve that, by the grace of God, you will continue to live as God's beloved child.

In most traditions, evening prayer comes soon after dinner but two or more hours before bedtime. At certain times, it is necessary to combine evening prayer with prayers at bedtime, and you may do so with this guide as well. Whatever the daily necessity, the aim is to bring your day to a close by recalling the ways God has been with you, by receiving the assurance of God's forgiveness, and by ending your day in God's peace.

When you are ready, find your accustomed devotional place or another suitable location for this time of prayer and use these words to express your gratitude to God:

Sunday: As the Lord's Day draws to a close, I thank you, O God, for the privilege of keeping sabbath through worship and rest.

Monday: As another day of work ends, I thank you, O God, that the abilities you have given me have been employed in ways that honor you.

Tuesday: At the close of this day, I thank you, O God, for all those who have contributed to the enrichment of my life.

Wednesday: As the day comes to an end, I thank you, O God, for the beauty and wonder of your creation.

Thursday: As the light of day recedes, I thank you, O God, that you are my light and my salvation.

Friday: As the business of the day evolves into the quietness of the evening, I thank you, O God, for the peace that you shed abroad in my heart.

Saturday: As the sun sets in anticipation of the Lord's Day tomorrow, I thank you, O God, for preparing my heart to worship you aright tomorrow.

The Invitatory

O God come to our assistance.
O God, hurry to save us.
O God, hasten to help us.

Glory be to the Father, and to the Son, and to the Holy Spirit; as it was in the beginning, is now, and will be forever. Amen.

Hymn of the Day

Sing again the hymn appointed for today (pages 35–98).

Psalm of the Day

Pray again the psalm appointed for today, perhaps in another translation (page 34).

Reading of the Evening

Read according to any plan you choose; sometimes persons use the evening to read books other than the Bible, especially devotional classics. This might be a good time to employ the Instructions from the Saints (pages 99–123).

Recollection of the Evening

Review your day. Thank God for giving you grace to live faithfully. Confess where you have failed to do so and ask for forgiveness. Resolve to make amends and live henceforth as God's beloved child.

Benediction

May the peace of God, which surpasses all understanding, guard your heart and your mind in Christ Jesus. Amen. (based on Phil. 4:7)

5.

PRAYER AT BEDTIME

PRAYER AT BEDTIME (often called Compline) is for the purpose of relinquishing the day to God and asking for God's care as we sleep. We close the door and place all things, including ourselves, in God's hands. We cannot go back, but we can move forward with the benefits of what we have learned in living today and with the assurance that God's grace is sufficient. There's no better way to end the day than confident of our safety in the arms of God.

As you approach your bedtime or as you lie in your bed before going to sleep, pray to God, asking for peace:

God, grant me a peaceful night and a perfect end. Amen.

Affirmation of Confidence

My help is in the name of the LORD, maker of heaven and earth.

Prayer of Relinquishment

Into your hands, O God, I commit my spirit. The day which you have given to me is now past. I thank you for the gift of life and the opportunity to glorify you today through my thoughts, words, and deeds. I leave today in your hands, trusting that you will take its successes and failures and weave them into a tapestry of love and grace for me and for those with whom I have come in contact. I especially pray for (   ), and I ask for your mercy, particularly in relation to (   ). Amen.

Benediction

I will both lie down and sleep in peace; for you alone, O LORD, make me lie down in safety (Ps. 4:8).

PSALM OF THE DAY

ALL PRAYER BOOKS true to the Christian tradition provide a way to pray the Psalms. Roman Catholic, Orthodox, and Protestant traditions all include the daily praying of the Psalms in some form. As we pray these passages of scripture, we join with ancient ancestors and contemporary pilgrims. The Psalms enable us to express a total range of emotions, to experience the full nature of God, and to practice a complete theology of prayer.

The simple schedule put forward here follows the months of the year, with one psalm read on the day that corresponds to its number.

In this way, you'll read through the books of Psalms and Proverbs twice in a year.

January and July	Psalms 1–30
February and August	Psalms 31–60
March and September	Psalms 61–90
April and October	Psalms 91–120
May and November	Psalms 121–150
June and December	Proverbs

HYMN AND PRAYER OF THE DAY

WE ARE MADE TO SING, and for three thousand years we have sung to God in our worship in the Judeo-Christian tradition. As we sing, we give expression to the full range of who God is and who we are. No truth or sentiment is left out of expressive singing.

John Wesley once referred to "hymns and other prayers," clearly including singing as a form of prayer. Similarly, the Te Decet Laus, a short doxological prayer, declares: "It is right to praise you, it is right to hymn you."

The hymns and prayers in this section are set together by day. In this way you can weave together your singing and praying. As you're able, use a hymnal and sing all the stanzas of the particular hymn. If a hymnal is not available, use the following excerpts. Sing out loud if you can; but if that's not possible, sing to God in your heart.

Prayer is the primary spiritual discipline. John Wesley called it one of the chief means of grace, the lack of which could not be made up for by any of the other means. Prayer is the way we establish and deepen our relationship with God, individually and corporately.

I have followed the weekly pattern that John Wesley and the early Methodists used in composing prayers for this section. A four-week cycle is presented with the following daily emphases:

Sunday	The Love of God
Monday	The Love of Neighbor
Tuesday	Humility
Wednesday	Self-Denial
Thursday	Meekness

| Friday | The Passion of Christ |
| Saturday | Gratitude |

You will find parentheses here and there in the daily prayers. Wesley used the parentheses as a way to encourage extemporaneous petitions within the framework of written prayer. I urge you to use the parentheses as "sacred space" to personalize your praying. And remember, written prayers are not read; they are prayed. Whether off the page or out of the mind, all prayer can be from the heart.

The hymn and prayer for each day are set together to facilitate their devotional use.

Week One: Sunday

Love divine, all loves excelling,
    joy of heaven, to earth come down;
fix in us thy humble dwelling;
    all thy faithful mercies crown!
Jesus, thou art all compassion,
    pure, unbounded love thou art;

visit us with thy salvation;
    Enter every trembling heart.

Breathe, O breathe thy loving Spirit
    into every troubled breast!
Let us all in thee inherit;
    let us find that second rest.
Take away our bent to sinning;
    Alpha and Omega be;
end of faith, as its beginning,
    set our hearts at liberty.

Come, Almighty to deliver,
    let us all thy life receive;
suddenly return and never,
    nevermore thy temples leave.
Thee we would be always blessing,
    serve thee as thy hosts above,
pray and praise thee without ceasing,
    glory in thy perfect love.

Finish, then, thy new creation;
    pure and spotless let us be.

Let us see thy great salvation
    perfectly restored in thee;
changed from glory into glory,
    till in heaven we take our place,
till we cast our crowns before thee,
    lost in wonder, love, and praise.

Charles Wesley, 1747

GRACIOUS GOD, your commandment to love you with all my heart, soul, mind, and strength is rooted in your prior love to me, expressed most fully in Jesus Christ. Knowing that I am your beloved child fills me with gratitude and encourages me to fulfill your command in every way I possibly can. Today, I am particularly grateful to be the recipient of your love in relation to (   ).

Assist me in every way by your grace, that as I live today, I may do so in a way that reveals and confirms my love for you. Give me unheralded opportunities to reflect your love as I move through the details of my life. Especially, increase the fruit of your Spirit: love, joy, peace, patience, kindness, goodness, faithfulness, gentleness, and self-control. I ask this in Jesus' name. Amen.

Week One: Monday

O Master, let me walk with thee
    in lowly paths of service free;
tell me thy secret; help me bear
    the strain of toil, the fret of care.

Help me the slow of heart to move
    by some clear, winning word of love;
teach me the wayward feet to stay,
    and guide them in the homeward way.

Teach me thy patience; still with thee
    in closer, dearer company,
in work that keeps faith sweet and strong,
    in trust that triumphs over wrong;

In hope that sends a shining ray
    far down the future's broadening way,

in peace that only thou canst give,

    with thee, O Master, let me live.

Washington Gladden, 1879

GOD OF ALL PEOPLE, thank you for reminding me that running a close second to my love for you is my love for others. You have commanded me to love my neighbor as I love myself. That is not difficult to understand, because I so easily see how many ways I love myself and look after my personal welfare.

Give me your grace today to extend this kind of love to others: to the people I know and those I do not know. Especially, give me grace to love (   ).

Make me as likely to love the stranger as I am to love my dearest friends. Enable me to love those who cross my path by surprise, as well as those who do so through the well-made plans of my day. In doing this, I bring honor to your name. And I desire to do this more than anything else in the world. In Jesus' name. Amen.

Week One: Tuesday

Just as I am, without one plea,
    but that thy blood was shed for me,
and that thou bidst me come to thee,
    O Lamb of God, I come, I come.

Just as I am, and waiting not
    to rid my soul of one dark blot,
to thee whose blood can cleanse each spot,
    O Lamb of God, I come, I come.

Just as I am, though tossed about
    with many a conflict, many a doubt,
fightings and fears within, without,
    O Lamb of God, I come, I come.

Just as I am, poor, wretched, blind;
    sight, riches, healing of the mind,
yea, all I need in thee to find,
    O Lamb of God, I come, I come.

Just as I am, thou wilt receive,
    wilt welcome, pardon, cleanse, relieve;

because thy promise I believe,
    O Lamb of God, I come, I come!

Just as I am, thy love unknown
    hath broken every barrier down;
now, to be thine, yea, thine alone,
    O Lamb of God, I come, I come.

Charlotte Elliott, 1835

ALMIGHTY GOD, I come to you as your unworthy servant, presenting myself in all humility. When I compare your love to me with mine to you, I realize how much and how often I fail to be the person you want me to be. I am without excuse, but I am not without appeal. I cry out today as I have so many times before: receive me into your presence, forgive me of my sins, and heal me of my faults. Today, I especially ask you to deal with (   ) in my life.

I ask this in the confidence that, for the sake of Christ, you will do it. I ask it with the remembrance of the many times in the past you have

done so. I glorify you for your complete goodness and mercy, which have followed me all the
days of my life and which I am sure will never
fail me as long as I live. Even as you have awak-
ened my body from sleep, so awaken my soul
unto everlasting life. In Jesus' name. Amen.

Week One: Wednesday

I want a principle within
　　of watchful, godly fear,
a sensibility of sin,
　　a pain to feel it near.
I want the first approach to feel
　　of pride or wrong desire,
to catch the wandering of my will,
　　and quench the kindling fire.

From thee that I no more may stray,
　　no more thy goodness grieve,
grant me the filial awe, I pray,
　　the tender conscience give.

Quick as the apple of an eye,
    O God, my conscience make;
awake my soul when sin is nigh,
    and keep it still awake.

Almighty God of truth and love,
    to me thy power impart;
the mountain from my soul remove,
    the hardness from my heart.
O may the least omission pain
    my reawakened soul,
and drive me to that blood again,
    which makes the wounded whole.

Charles Wesley, 1749

DEAR GOD, my number one problem is me. I have embraced a false self that tries in every way to tell me *I* am in control—and even more dangerously, tells me not to trust you but rather to trust in my own alleged righteousness. I am ashamed at how many times I have listened to the voice of the false self instead of your voice.

Today, I deny that false self and ask that you would renew a right spirit within me, a self that attends to you and lives accordingly. Especially today, I ask that I might deny the false self in relation to (   ). I am tired of going where it leads me. Instead, lead me in paths of righteousness for your name's sake. I ask this in Jesus' name. Amen.

Week One: Thursday

Alas! and did my Savior bleed,
    and did my Sovereign die?
Would he devote that sacred head
    for sinners such as I?

Was it for crimes that I have done,
    he groaned upon the tree?
Amazing pity! Grace unknown!
    And love beyond degree!

Well might the sun in darkness hide,
    and shut its glories in,

when God, the mighty maker, died
    for his own creature's sin.

Thus might I hide my blushing face
    while his dear cross appears;
dissolve my heart in thankfulness,
    and melt mine eyes to tears.

But drops of tears can ne'er repay
    the debt of love I owe.
Here, Lord, I give myself away;
    'tis all that I can do.

Isaac Watts, 1707

GUIDING GOD, I desire to live in meekness before you this day. I understand that to be meek is not to be weak but rather to be under your control. You have created every person with amazing potential, but that power in human hands turns into a problem and a pain. Only in your hands do we discover the right use of our lives.

Like a horse that submits itself to its rider through the bridle, I submit to your guidance through the promptings of your Spirit and the exercise of my conscience. If to the right or left I stray, convict me and bring me back upon the path you will for me. Today, I particularly feel the need for your guidance in (   ).

Give me the mind that was in Christ, namely the disposition of my life to want only what you want and to move in that direction when I understand what that is. Amen.

Week One: Friday

When I survey the wondrous cross
    on which the Prince of Glory died,
my richest gain I count but loss,
    and pour contempt on all my pride.

Forbid it, Lord, that I should boast,
    save in the death of Christ, my God;
all the vain things that charm me most,
    I sacrifice them to his blood.

See, from his head, his hands, his feet,
    sorrow and love flow mingled down.
Did e'er such love and sorrow meet,
    or thorns compose so rich a crown?

Were the whole realm of nature mine,
    that were an offering far too small;
love so amazing, so divine,
    demands my soul, my life, my all.

Isaac Watts, 1707

HOLY FATHER, on this day when Jesus went to the cross for our redemption—for *my* redemption—I come to you with gratitude that I can never fully put into words. By sending Christ to be the Savior of the world, you have delivered my soul from sin and death and given me the assured hope of eternal life. By his stripes I have been healed!

Work out the benefits of the Atonement in my life this day, specifically in relation to (   ), that by your grace I may no longer live in the bondage to sin that comes when I prefer my way instead of yours. Knowing that I deserve punishment but instead receive mercy, I bow my heart before you asking that you would search me thoroughly and wherever you find any hurtful thing, you will apply redeeming grace in that place. I ask this in the name of Jesus. Amen.

Week One: Saturday

O for a thousand tongues to sing
    my great Redeemer's praise,
the glories of my God and King,
    the triumphs of his grace!

My gracious Master and my God,
    assist me to proclaim,
to spread through all the earth abroad
    the honors of thy name.

Jesus! the name that charms our fears,
    that bids our sorrows cease;

'tis music in the sinner's ears,
    'tis life, and health, and peace.

He breaks the power of canceled sin,
    he sets the prisoner free;
his blood can make the foulest clean;
    his blood availed for me.

He speaks, and listening to his voice,
    new life the dead receive;
the mournful, broken hearts rejoice,
    the humble poor believe.

In Christ, your head, you then shall know,
    shall feel your sins forgiven;
anticipate your heaven below,
    and own that love is heaven.

Charles Wesley, 1739

BLESSED GOD, I use this day as an occasion to look back upon the week I have lived. In doing so, I trace the footprints of your presence with me. I have seen you at work in the little things and the big things that have happened. I am particularly mindful of your goodness in relation to (   ). When I count my blessings, naming them one by one, it is wonderful to see all that you have done.

Set me free from the temptation to grovel in my failures and also save me from any presumptions that would keep me from taking them seriously. It is in the space between despair and pride that I need you to work most in my life.

And what I ask for myself, I ask for others, especially (   ). I ask all this in Jesus' name. Amen.

Week Two: Sunday

Joyful, joyful, we adore thee,
     God of glory, Lord of love;
hearts unfold like flowers before thee,
     opening to the sun above.
Melt the clouds of sin and sadness;
     drive the dark of doubt away.

Giver of immortal gladness,
    fill us with the light of day!

All thy works with joy surround thee,
    earth and heaven reflect thy rays,
stars and angels sing around thee,
    center of unbroken praise.
Field and forest, vale and mountain,
    flowery meadow, flashing sea,
chanting bird and flowing fountain,
    call us to rejoice in thee.

Thou art giving and forgiving,
    ever blessing, ever blest,
wellspring of the joy of living,
    ocean depth of happy rest!
Thou our Father, Christ our brother,
    all who live in love are thine;
teach us how to love each other,
    lift us to the joy divine.

Mortals, join the mighty chorus
    which the morning stars began;

love divine is reigning o'er us,
>   binding all within its span.
Ever singing, march we onward,
>   victors in the midst of strife;
joyful music leads us sunward,
>   in the triumph song of life.

Henry Van Dyke, 1907

O GOD, you who are love, fill my soul with an
entire love of you, so that I may love nothing
for any other reason than your glory. Incline my
heart so that I may both receive your love and,
in turn, be an agent of it.

Give me grace to organize my whole life in
relation to your love. Motivate me to read your
Word, so that I may comprehend more about
your love. Inspire me to pray throughout this
day, so that what I know can be applied to the
specific circumstances of my life, particularly
(   ). I want to be a doer of your Word, not
just a hearer of it.

And what I ask for this day, I also ask for the rest of my life, so that even on my dying day I may be found to be your beloved child and a faithful conveyor of that love to others. In Jesus' name. Amen.

Week Two: Monday

Happy the home when God is there,
    and love fills every breast;
when one their wish, and one their prayer,
    and one their heavenly rest.

Happy the home where Jesus' name
    is sweet to every ear;
where children early speak his fame,
    and parents hold him dear.

Happy the home where prayer is heard,
    and praise is wont to rise;
where parents love the sacred Word
    and all its wisdom prize.

Lord, let us in our homes agree
    this blessed peace to gain;
unite our hearts in love to thee,
    and love to all will reign.

Henry Ware Jr., 1846

PROTECTING GOD, defend me against the temptations of this life, so that I may not knowingly prefer my will to yours, and in so doing bring harm to anyone with whom I come in contact today. And should I do so anyway, make me quick to realize my sin and to repent of it—making amends as is appropriate with those I have harmed. Do not allow my faults to accumulate and contaminate my soul.

Make me zealous to use every occasion I have today as an opportunity to increase the happiness of others and relieve their suffering, especially in relation to (   ). Even as Jesus embodied your love to others, use my body today to honor you. Make me an instrument of your peace. I ask this in Jesus' name. Amen.

Week Two: Tuesday

And can it be that I should gain
    an interest in the Savior's blood!
Died he for me? who caused his pain!
    For me? who him to death pursued?
Amazing love! How can it be
    that thou, my God, shouldst die for me?

'Tis mystery all: th'Immortal dies!
    Who can explore his strange design?
In vain the firstborn seraph tries
    to sound the depths of love divine.
'Tis mercy all! Let earth adore;
    let angel minds inquire no more.

He left his Father's throne above
    (so free, so infinite his grace!),
emptied himself of all but love,
    and bled for Adam's helpless race.
'Tis mercy all, immense and free,
    for O my God, it found out me!

Long my imprisoned spirit lay,
     fast bound in sin and nature's night;
thine eye diffused a quickening ray;
     I woke, the dungeon flamed with light;
my chains fell off, my heart was free,
     I rose, went forth, and followed thee.

No condemnation now I dread;
     Jesus, and all in him, is mine;
alive in him, my living Head,
     and clothed in righteousness divine,
bold I approach th'eternal throne,
     and claim the crown, through Christ my own.

Charles Wesley, 1739

O GOD, teach me the way of Christ, who humbled himself and became obedient, even to the point of death upon the cross. Shed your light on my life; illumine all within me that would destroy humility, the hallmark of love. Let me walk in the light that comes when I remember you are God, and I am not.

I give you myself today, and I do so willingly and without reservation. Take me as I am, make me what I need to be, and then use me in whatever ways you see fit. I understand that I am in your hands, and they are good hands. I realize that you will never send me where your grace will not be sufficient. In that assurance, I am happy to be your servant in all things and especially in (   ). In Jesus' name. Amen.

Week Two: Wednesday

Take my life, and let it be
    consecrated, Lord, to thee.
Take my moments and my days;
    let them flow in ceaseless praise.
Take my hands, and let them move
    at the impulse of thy love.
Take my feet, and let them be
    swift and beautiful for thee.

Take my voice, and let me sing
    always, only, for my King.

Take my lips, and let them be
    filled with messages from thee.
Take my silver and my gold;
    not a mite would I withhold.
Take my intellect, and use
    every power as thou shalt choose.

Take my will, and make it thine;
    it shall be no longer mine.
Take my heart, it is thine own;
    it shall be thy royal throne.
Take my love, my Lord, I pour
    at thy feet its treasure store.
Take myself, and I will be
    ever, only, all for thee.

Frances R. Havergal, 1873

DEAR GOD, when I pray "thy kingdom come,
thy will be done on earth, as it is in heaven," I
choose to reject everything in me and around
me that would keep that from happening. I
realize I am denying myself the right to reign

and rule and asking that you and you alone will reign and rule in me. Today, I especially sense my need for self-denial in relation to (   ).

Even when I do not enact my desire perfectly, I run to you, knowing that you will receive me to yourself, forgiving me and healing me, so that my defects will not continue to control me. You know my heart; I want you to own me today. May that ownership produce singleness of heart and life in me. In Jesus' name. Amen.

Week Two: Thursday

There is a place of quiet rest,
    near to the heart of God;
a place where sin cannot molest,
    near to the heart of God.
O Jesus, blest Redeemer,
    sent from the heart of God,
hold us who wait before thee
    near to the heart of God.

There is a place of comfort sweet,
    near to the heart of God;
a place where we our Savior meet,
    near to the heart of God.
O Jesus, blest Redeemer,
    sent from the heart of God,
hold us who wait before thee
    near to the heart of God.

There is a place of full release,
    near to the heart of God;
a place where all is joy and peace,
    near to the heart of God.
O Jesus, blest Redeemer,
    sent from the heart of God,
hold us who wait before thee
    near to the heart of God.

Cleland B. McAfee, 1903

O GOD, give me a teachable spirit, reminding me that to be a true disciple is to adopt literally the spirit of a learner. Show me how much I have yet to learn, not to discourage but to inspire me to be a person who passionately pursues whatever you want me to know. Save me from ever convincing myself that I have "arrived" and that I can now rest and take my ease—which is to settle for the false security of pseudocompetence.

And as you inspire me to learn and grow, give me the desire to put what I learn into practice for the sake of others. I recognize my responsibilities in this regard for these persons ( ). I earnestly desire that your wisdom might flow through me to them and that it might do so in a way that causes them to focus on you, not me. I ask this in Jesus' name. Amen.

Week Two: Friday

Were you there when they crucified my Lord?
　　Were you there when they crucified my Lord?
Oh! sometimes it causes me to tremble, tremble,
　　　　tremble.
　　Were you there when they crucified my Lord?

Were you there when they nailed him to the
tree?

>Were you there when they nailed him to the
tree?

Oh! sometimes it causes me to tremble, tremble,
tremble.

>Were you there when they nailed him to the
tree?

Were you there when they pierced him in the
side?

>Were you there when they pierced him in
the side?

Oh! sometimes it causes me to tremble, tremble,
tremble.

>Were you there when they pierced him in
the side?

Were you there when the sun refused to shine?

>Were you there when the sun refused to
shine?

Oh! sometimes it causes me to tremble, tremble,
tremble.

Were you there when the sun refused to
shine?

Were you there when they laid him in the tomb?

Were you there when they laid him in the
tomb?

Oh! sometimes it causes me to tremble, tremble,
tremble.

Were you there when they laid him in the
tomb?

Afro-American Spiritual, no date

HEAVENLY FATHER, on a Friday your Son went
to the cross to die for me, so that I can live for
you. Despite his suffering and death—indeed,
through it—we can truly call today a "good Friday." I acknowledge that this goodness becomes
activated in me only as I recognize my need for
salvation in Christ and open myself to receive it
as a grace gift from you.

Today I declare my commitment to you using the words of a hymn: "Lord, I want to be a Christian in my heart." I have heard your knock upon the door of my heart and again today—God willing, every day—I go to that door and open it, ready to receive any word you might have for me (   ). In Jesus' name. Amen.

Week Two: Saturday

For the beauty of the earth,
    for the glory of the skies,
for the love which from our birth
    over and around us lies;
Lord of all, to thee we raise
    this our hymn of grateful praise.

For the beauty of each hour
    of the day and of the night,
hill and vale, and tree and flower,
    sun and moon, and stars of light;
Lord of all, to thee we raise
    this our hymn of grateful praise.

For the joy of ear and eye,
    for the heart and mind's delight,
for the mystic harmony
    linking sense to sound and sight;
Lord of all, to thee we raise
    this our hymn of grateful praise.

For the joy of human love,
    brother, sister, parent, child,
friends on earth and friends above,
    for all gentle thoughts and mild;
Lord of all, to thee we raise
    this our hymn of grateful praise.

For thy church, that evermore
    lifteth holy hands above,
offering upon every shore
    her pure sacrifice of love;
Lord of all, to thee we raise
    this our hymn of grateful praise.

For thyself, best Gift Divine,
    to the world so freely given,

for that great, great love of thine,
    peace on earth, and joy in heaven:
Lord of all, to thee we raise
    this our hymn of grateful praise.

Folliot S. Pierpoint, 1864

O GOD, today I join with Christians of the ages, in thanking you for the privilege of worship, the central act of the people of God. I join with members of the church invisible and visible in asking you to prepare my heart to worship you aright tomorrow. I grasp that I cannot do this on the spot and that these hours leading up to Sunday are critical in enabling me to enter your gates with thanksgiving and your courts with praise.

I pray also that you will anoint the clergy and laity who will be involved in the conduct of that worship, especially (   ). As they put the finishing touches on their messages and draw nearer to their acts of service, may they too be deepened in their desire to worship you in spirit and in truth. I ask this in Jesus' name. Amen.

Week Three: Sunday

All hail the power of Jesus' name!
    Let angels prostrate fall;
bring forth the royal diadem,
    and crown him Lord of all.
Bring forth the royal diadem,
    and crown him Lord of all.

Ye chosen seed of Israel's race,
    ye ransomed from the fall,
hail him who saves you by his grace,
    and crown him Lord of all.
Hail him who saves you by his grace,
    and crown him Lord of all.

Sinners, whose love can ne'er forget
    the wormwood and the gall,
go spread your trophies at his feet,
    and crown him Lord of all.
Go spread your trophies at his feet,
    and crown him Lord of all.

Let every kindred, every tribe
    on this terrestrial ball,
to him all majesty ascribe,
    and crown him Lord of all.
To him all majesty ascribe,
    and crown him Lord of all.

O that with yonder sacred throng
    we at his feet may fall!
We'll join the everlasting song,
    and crown him Lord of all.
We'll join the everlasting song,
    and crown him Lord of all.

Edward Perronet, 1779; alt. by John Rippon, 1787

GOD OF LOVE, I rise from sleep to adore your holy name, presenting myself to you with thanksgiving for all your mercies. I glorify you, Father, for creating me and all that is. I glorify you, blessed Son, for being my Savior, guardian, and friend. I glorify you, Holy Spirit, for indwelling me and guiding me in the ways of faith.

Give me grace this day to walk in your ways, doing so in a way that sets me on your path for the rest of my life. Establish me in a pattern of true devotion, particularly in relation to (   ). I know you desire more from me than days of devotion here and there—moments of faithfulness now and then. In that knowledge, I offer to love you now and always. Amen.

Week Three: Monday

Forth in thy name, O Lord, I go,
    my daily labor to pursue;
thee, only thee, resolved to know
    in all I think or speak or do.

The task thy wisdom hath assigned,
    O let me cheerfully fulfill;
in all my works thy presence find,
    and prove thy good and perfect will.

Thee may I set at my right hand,
    whose eyes mine inmost substance see,

and labor on at thy command,
    and offer all my works to thee.

For thee delightfully employ
    whate'er thy bounteous grace hath given;
and run my course with even joy,
    and closely walk with thee to heaven.

Charles Wesley, 1749

DEAR GOD, I acknowledge that as part of the human family, everyone is truly my neighbor. I do not live for myself only; save me from ever thinking or acting as if I do. Make me conscious of my place in the human family. May I live in love and service with all persons.

May I never fail to see opportunities to love that are near to me, especially in relation to (   ). Help me order my life in simplicity and stewardship, so that I contribute to the welfare of those who live beyond my reach. I ask this for myself and especially for those devoted to ministries of justice and mercy. Amen.

Week Three: Tuesday

Breathe on me, Breath of God,
    fill me with life anew,
that I may love what thou dost love,
    and do what thou wouldst do.

Breathe on me, Breath of God,
    until my heart is pure,
until with thee I will one will,
    to do and to endure.

Breathe on me, Breath of God,
    till I am wholly thine,
till all this earthly part of me
    glows with thy fire divine.

Breathe on me, Breath of God,
    so shall I never die,
but live with thee the perfect life
    of thine eternity.

Edwin Hatch, 1878

ALMIGHTY GOD, one of your best gifts is your reminder that you are God, and I am not. My ego seizes upon every opportunity to exalt and enlarge itself. I have wrestled with pride over the years of my life and most recently in relation to (   ). I need a work of grace that tends my soul toward humility.

I acknowledge your decision to extend this grace directly by your Holy Spirit or indirectly through the circumstances of my life this day. I open myself to both means of your grace. And I affirm that however you choose to increase humility in me, you do so for my good and your glory. In that confidence, I move into my day as your beloved child. In Jesus' name. Amen.

Week Three: Wednesday

Come, sinners, to the gospel feast;
    let every soul be Jesus' guest.
Ye need not one be left behind,
    for God hath bid all humankind.

Sent by my Lord, on you I call;
　　the invitation is to all.
Come, all the world! Come sinner, thou!
　　All things in Christ are ready now.

Come, all ye souls by sin oppressed,
　　ye restless wanderers after rest;
ye poor, and maimed, and halt, and blind,
　　in Christ a hearty welcome find.

My message as from God receive;
　　ye all may come to Christ and live.
O let his love your hearts constrain,
　　nor suffer him to die in vain.
This is the time, no more delay!
　　This is the Lord's accepted day.
Come thou, this moment, at his call,
　　and live for him who died for all.

Charles Wesley, 1747

DEAR GOD, you know me better than I know myself—inside and out, top to bottom. You know when I rise up and when I lie down. You are acquainted with all my ways. You can detect the emergence of pride and self-will long before I can. I ask you to deal with me in the inner chambers of my life, so that my false self can be checked at the earliest possible moment.

And even as you do this, I recognize that you use my own faculties to foster my awareness of my need for self-denial. In this moment, I am conscious of that need in (   ). Deliver me from this and any other evil that becomes apparent to me today. O God, come to my assistance. Hurry to help me. Hasten to save me. I ask this in Jesus' name. Amen.

Week Three: Thursday

Take time to be holy,
    speak oft with thy Lord;
abide in him always,
    and feed on his word.
Make friends of God's children,
    help those who are weak,

forgetting in nothing
　　　his blessing to seek.

Take time to be holy,
　　　the world rushes on;
spend much time in secret
　　　with Jesus alone.
By looking to Jesus,
　　　like him thou shalt be;
thy friends in thy conduct
　　　his likeness shall see.
Take time to be holy,
　　　let him be thy guide,
and run not before him,
　　　whatever betide.
In joy or in sorrow,
　　　still follow the Lord,
and, looking to Jesus,
　　　still trust in his word.

Take time to be holy,
　　　be calm in thy soul,

each thought and each motive
    beneath his control.
Thus led by his spirit
    to fountains of love,
thou soon shalt be fitted
    for service above.

William D. Longstaff, ca. 1882

FRUIT-BEARING GOD, if meekness is "power under control," give me love, joy, peace, patience, kindness, goodness, faithfulness, gentleness, and self-control—which individually and together move me into greater conformity to Christ, the ultimate and perfect example of meekness. Today, I particularly feel the need for an increase of the fruit of ( ) in my life.

Just as all of Christ's power was at your disposal, I willingly give you permission to use my life in whatever way you see fit today. I believe it is right to want my life to count, but I want it to count for you. So, bring me under your control in ways that will make your will and my will one and the same. This too is the example Christ has given to me through his prayer, "not my will, but thine, be done" (KJV). Give me that desire. I ask this in his name. Amen.

Week Three: Friday

Jesus, keep me near the cross;
    there a precious fountain,
free to all, a healing stream,
    flows from Calvary's mountain.

Refrain: In the cross, in the cross,
    be my glory ever,
till my raptured soul shall find
    rest beyond the river.

Near the cross, a trembling soul,
    love and mercy found me;
there the bright and morning star
    sheds its beams around me.

Refrain

Near the cross! O Lamb of God,
  bring its scenes before me;
help me walk from day to day
  with its shadow o'er me.

Refrain

Near the cross I'll watch and wait,
  hoping, trusting, ever,
till I reach the golden strand
  just beyond the river.

Refrain

Fanny J. Crosby, 1869

CREATOR GOD, in ways I do not fully under-stand, Christ's atonement brings salvation to the whole creation, not just to human beings. But along with people, the whole creation still groans for its final deliverance from sin. I accept the fact that I am commissioned to be an instrument in your hands to care for the earth in ways that move it closer to its ultimate redemption.

I pray that all people might catch the vision of their place in this ecological mission, and I pray particularly for those who work daily in vocations that care for the earth (   ). Give me grace to keep my part of the world clean, knowing that if everyone did this, we would find ourselves on a much different planet. In Jesus' name I pray. Amen.

Week Three: Saturday

O sacred Head, now wounded,
    with grief and shame weighed down,
now scornfully surrounded
    with thorns, thine only crown:
how pale thou art with anguish,
    with sore abuse and scorn!
How dost that visage languish
    which once was bright as morn!

What thou, my Lord, hast suffered
    was all for sinners' gain;
mine, mine was the transgression,

but thine the deadly pain.
Lo, here I fall, my Savior!
    'Tis I deserve thy place;
look on me with thy favor,
    vouchsafe to me thy grace.

What language shall I borrow
    to thank thee, dearest friend,
for this thy dying sorrow,
    thy pity without end?
O make me thine forever;
    and should I fainting be,
Lord, let me never, never
    outlive my love to thee.

Anonymous, Latin;
Translated by Paul Gerhardt, 1656,
and James W. Alexander, 1830

DEAR GOD, I can think of no greater folly than to consider myself a self-made person. Today I remember how interconnected my life has been, is, and will be—with untold numbers of persons who directly and indirectly contribute to my well-being. I pray for those in my network of family and friends who support me in their prayers (   ), and I pray for those I do not know and may never know, who also labor to make my life better. I think today particularly of those who (   ).

In giving thanks for them, give me your grace to reverse the process and be one who benefits others, both near and far away—known and unknown. Show me how I may do this in my life and in my work. Fill my life with gratitude for having received so much from others and for having the opportunity to give much to them. I ask this in Jesus' name. Amen.

Week Four: Sunday

More love to thee, O Christ,
    more love to thee!
Hear thou the prayer I make
    on bended knee.

This is my earnest plea:
    More love, O Christ, to thee;
more love to thee,
    more love to thee!

Once earthly joy I craved,
    sought peace and rest;
now thee alone I seek,
    give what is best.
This all my prayer shall be:
    More love, O Christ, to thee;
more love to thee,
    more love to thee!

Let sorrow do its work,
    come grief and pain;
sweet are thy messengers,
    sweet their refrain,
when they can sing with me:
    More love, O Christ, to thee;
more love to thee,
    more love to thee!

Then shall my latest breath
 whisper thy praise;
this be the parting cry
 my heart shall raise;
this still its prayer shall be:
 More love, O Christ, to thee;
more love to thee,
 more love to thee!

Elizabeth P. Prentiss, 1869

GOD OF ALL LOVE, your love for me and for the whole creation is beyond anything I can imagine. Your thoughts are not my thoughts, and your ways are not my ways. But the immensity of your love does not frighten me; it encourages me. For if I could fully fathom your love and live in it, it would be no bigger than I am. And I need a love at work me in me that is infinitely larger than that, particularly with respect to ( ).

I give you myself today as completely as I can, knowing that the experience of your love will create an even greater openness to you in the days to come. Choose for me the best expression of your love as I live today, and I will gladly receive it, as well as seek to find ways to share it with others. In Jesus' name. Amen.

Week Four: Monday

Jesus, united by thy grace
    and each to each endeared,
with confidence we seek thy face
    and know our prayer is heard.

Help us to help each other, Lord,
    each other's cross to bear;
let all their friendly aid afford,
    and feel each other's care.

Up unto thee, our living Head,
    let us in all things grow;
till thou hast made us free indeed
    and spotless here below.

Touched by the lodestone of thy love,
    let all our hearts agree,

and ever toward each other move,
    and ever move toward thee.

To thee, inseparably joined,
    let all our spirits cleave;
O may we all the loving mind
    that was in thee receive.

This is the bond of perfectness,
    thy spotless charity;
O let us, still we pray, possess
    the mind that was in thee.

Charles Wesley, 1742

RECONCILING GOD, I don't like to believe that I actually have enemies, but I acknowledge that I am not in the best of relations with all my friends and acquaintances. I'm thinking today of ( ). Today I accept Jesus' command to "love your enemies" as applying to this person. Forgive me where I have failed to be a neighbor. Guide me into ways of living that will make our relationship more like what you want it to be.

As I do this close to home, I turn my heart to the nations of the world, asking that even though I live in a world where I'm told I have "friends" and "enemies," that I will reject such an evaluation in favor of realizing that, in Christ, I only have "brothers" and "sisters." I ask this in Jesus' name. Amen.

Week Four: Tuesday

O for a heart to praise my God,
    a heart from sin set free,
a heart that always feels thy blood
    so freely shed for me.

A heart resigned, submissive, meek,
    my great Redeemer's throne,
where only Christ is heard to speak,
    where Jesus reigns alone.

A humble, lowly, contrite heart,
    believing, true, and clean,
which neither life nor death can part
    from Christ who dwells within.

A heart in every thought renewed
    and full of love divine,
perfect and right and pure and good,
    a copy, Lord, of thine.

Thy nature, gracious Lord, impart;
    come quickly from above;
write thy new name upon my heart,
    thy new, best name of Love.

Charles Wesley, 1742

O Christ, I realize that comparing myself with others is the way of death, because my ego will quickly provide a list of persons to whom I think I'm superior. Forgive me for the pride that rises up when I make superficial and false comparisons. Forgive me for having done this in relation to (   ).

I also understand that the way of life is to compare myself with you. Immediately, I find humility rising up in me, and that is exactly what I need. I acknowledge that I can never be you, but I take great joy in knowing that I can be "like" you; indeed, that you have made me to be so. I accept that likeness in my relationship with you, while at the same time refusing to play God in relation to others. Amen.

Week Four: Wednesday

When we walk with the Lord
    in the light of his word,
what a glory he sheds on our way!
    While we do his good will,
he abides with us still,
    and with all who will trust and obey.

Refrain: Trust and obey,
    for there's no other way
to be happy in Jesus,
    but to trust and obey.

Not a burden we bear,
    not a sorrow we share,
but our toil he doth richly repay;

not a grief or a loss,
not a frown or a cross,
but is blest if we trust and obey.

Refrain

But we never can prove
the delights of his love
until all on the altar we lay;
for the favor he shows,
for the joy he bestows,
are for those who will trust and obey.

Refrain

Then in fellowship sweet
we will sit at his feet,
or we'll walk by his side in the way;
what he says we will do,
where he sends we will go;
never fear, only trust and obey.

Refrain

John H. Sammis, 1887

DEAR GOD, in denying myself, I realize that you only ask me to deny myself when that false self tries to convince me to live apart from you. You never ask me to deny myself as the unique and unrepeatable person you have made me to be. You do not ask me to cancel myself but rather to consecrate my life. Today, I do that in relation to ( ).

That is my desire today, and I pray it will always be. I want myself to be yours, not mine or anyone else's. I realize you have given me freedom of choice in relation to this. You have already voted for me. The evil forces of the world have voted against me. Today I will break the tie. Give me the grace to live this day in you. In Jesus' name. Amen.

Week Four: Thursday

O Love that wilt not let me go,
    I rest my weary soul in thee;
I give thee back the life I owe,

that in thine ocean depths its flow
may richer, fuller be.

O Light that followest all my way,
   I yield my flickering torch to thee;
my heart restores its borrowed ray,
   that in thy sunshine's blaze its day
may brighter, fairer be.

O Joy that seekest me through pain,
   I cannot close my heart to thee;
I trace the rainbow thru the rain,
   and feel the promise is not vain,
that morn shall tearless be.

O Cross that liftest up my head,
   I dare not ask to fly from thee;
I lay in dust life's glory dead,
   and from the ground there blossoms red
life that shall endless be.

George Matheson, 1882

HEAVENLY FATHER, when I pray for meekness, I understand that I am praying for the mind that was in your Son. I am not praying for an isolated characteristic of my life but rather a total disposition of my heart: the spirit that was in Jesus, who asked that his entire spirit, soul, and body would be under your control. From that place, he did what he knew would please you; and he found joy in doing so.

As I think about how you have guided me in the past, I am strengthened in my desire for you to do so today and assured that as I seek to live in meekness, you will give me the grace to do so. I ask for this, and I am particularly aware of my need for it in relation to (   ). In Jesus' name. Amen.

Week Four: Friday

O Love divine, what hast thou done!
    The immortal God hath died for me!
The Father's coeternal Son

bore all my sins upon the tree.
Th'immortal God for me hath died:
  My Lord, my Love, is crucified!

Is crucified for me and you,
    to bring us rebels back to God.
Believe, believe the record true,
    ye all are bought with Jesus' blood.
Pardon for all flows from his side:
  My Lord, my Love, is crucified!
Behold him, all ye that pass by,
    the bleeding Prince of life and peace!
Come, sinners, see your Savior die,
    and say, "Was ever grief like his?"
Come, feel with me his blood applied:
  My Lord, my Love, is crucified!

Charles Wesley, 1742

SAVING GOD, I stand amazed when I consider that Jesus counted it all joy to go to the cross. On this day, when he did so, teach me to find joy in things I would tend to avoid or even reject. Forgive me for trying to define my Christian life in terms of the things that are pleasant, quick, and easy—especially in relation to (   ).

Teach me the joy of accomplishing your will when it can only be done through painful, slow, and challenging ways. Deliver me from a spirituality of entertainment, and replace it with one of engagement. Give me your graced ability to accept the sound of hosannas or the hammering of nails. In Jesus' name. Amen.

Week Four: Saturday

Holy, holy, holy!
    Lord God Almighty!
Early in the morning
    our song shall rise to thee.
Holy, holy, holy!
    Merciful and mighty,
God in three persons,
    blessed Trinity!

Holy, holy, holy!
    All the saints adore thee,

casting down their golden crowns
    around the glassy sea;
cherubim and seraphim
    falling down before thee,
which wert, and art,
    and evermore shalt be.

Holy, holy, holy!
    Though the darkness hide thee,
though the eye of sinful man
    thy glory may not see,
only thou art holy;
    there is none beside thee,
perfect in power
    in love and purity.

Holy, holy, holy!
    Lord God Almighty!
All thy works shall praise thy name,
    in earth and sky and sea.
Holy, holy, holy!
    Merciful and mighty,

God in three persons,
    blessed Trinity.

Reginald Heber, 1826

ETERNAL GOD, when I come to stand in your presence, my first word to you will be *thanks*. No longer seeing imperfectly and incompletely, I will stand amazed in your presence and will realize as never before your amazing goodness to me.

Train my soul in the ways of gratitude here and now. Let the days of my life become rehearsals for my ultimate thanksgiving in heaven. I pause to say thank you for as many things as tumble into my consciousness in this moment (   ). Help me see these things as a trajectory into the future, trusting that I will have as many reasons for gratitude in the future as I do today. In Jesus' name. Amen.

INSTRUCTIONS FROM THE SAINTS

APART FROM THE BIBLE, the witness of the saints provides us with our greatest instruction in the life of prayer. Far from being artificial and detached, these saints were ordinary Christians who practiced prayer in the same ways we do. From the second century AD until the present, these devoted men and women inspire and guide us. Their words become our "school of prayer." I have included this section as a means to further guide your formation. You can include these selections in your daily pattern as you desire.

This section opens with some statements about prayer that connect to Jesus' words in Matthew 6:5-8. Then we turn to the Lord's Prayer, which was viewed as a pattern for prayer as well as a prayer itself. Finally, we give some days to miscellaneous teachings that offer additional insights. In this way, we can unite with the "great cloud of witnesses" (Heb. 12:1, NIV) and allow the church invisible to enrich our praying until the day we become members of it.

The quotations in this section come from The Upper Room Spiritual Classics (series 1–3).

Week One: Day One

By the end of the fourth century, the deserts of the Near East were filled with tens of thousands of men and women, each of whom had heard the call of God to "flee, be silent, and pray." We call them the desert fathers and mothers. One of them, Amma Syncletica, believed prayer should be offered in deep humility

"Imitate the publican, and you will not be condemned with the Pharisee. Choose the meekness of Moses, and you will find your heart that is a rock changed into a spring of water."

Keith Beasley-Topliffe, ed., *Seeking a Purer Christian Life: Sayings and Stories of the Desert Mothers and Fathers*, Upper Room Spiritual Classics 3 (Nashville, TN: Upper Room Books, 2000), 57.

Week One: Day Two

One of the most beloved desert fathers was Macarius. Here is his response to "How should one pray?"

"There is no need at all to make long discourses; it is enough to stretch out one's hands and say, 'Lord, as you will, and as you know, have mercy.' And if the conflict grows fiercer, say, 'Lord, help!' God knows very well what we need and shows us mercy."

Ibid.

Week One: Day Three

Near the end of the fourth century, Saint Augustine became bishop of Hippo in Africa and a prominent leader and theologian of his day. When asked to comment on the need for prayer if God already knows what we need, he wrote:

"The very effort involved in prayer calms and purifies our heart, and makes it roomier for receiving the divine gifts that are poured into us spiritually. . . . God is always ready to give us light. . . . But we are not always ready to receive. . . . So prayer brings about a turning of the heart to God, who is ever ready to give, if we will but take what God has given. And in the very act of turning, there is effected a cleansing of the inner eye."

Keith Beasley-Topliffe, ed., *Hungering for God: Selected Writings of Augustine*, Upper Room Spiritual Classics 1 (Nashville, TN: Upper Room Books, 1997), 67–68.

Week One: Day Four

As a bishop, Augustine was responsible for instructing people who were to be baptized. After preaching on the Apostles' Creed, he would use the Lord's Prayer as a model for prayer, not simply as a prayer itself. Without hesitation, he emphasized the importance of the Lord's Prayer in the Christian life:

"The words that our Lord Jesus Christ has taught us in his prayer are the rule and standard of our desires. You may not ask for anything but what is written there.

". . . You are on the eve of being brought forth in the font, the womb as it were of the church. 'Our Father in heaven.' Remember then, that you have a Father in heaven . . . and that you are to be born again into [the] life of God."

Ibid., 69.

Week One: Day Five

We now turn for five days to a writing of Saint Francis of Assisi in the thirteenth century—a paraphrase of the Lord's Prayer. It shows how Christians have used the prayer as a model for their praying.

"*Our Father,* most holy, Creator, Redeemer, Savior,

Comforter, *in heaven,* in the angels and saints enlightening them to knowledge of you, for you, Lord, are Light; inflaming them to love of you, for you, Lord, are Love; dwelling in them and filling them with blessing, for you, Lord, are the highest good, the eternal good, from whom all good proceeds, without whom nothing is good."

Keith Beasley-Topliffe, ed., *The Riches of Simplicity: Selected Writings of Francis and Clare*, Upper Room Spiritual Classics 2 (Nashville, TN: Upper Room Books, 1998), 34.

Week One: Day Six

"*Hallowed be your name,* may it be glorified in us by knowledge of you, that we may perceive the wideness of your blessings, the extent of your promises, the height of your majesty, the depth of your judgments.

"*Your kingdom come,* that you may reign in us by your grace and bring us to your kingdom, where the vision of you is revealed, and your love made perfect, that we may enter your blessed presence, and enjoy you forever."

Ibid.

Week One: Day Seven

"Your will be done, on earth as in heaven, that we may love you with all our hearts, ever thinking of you, and desiring you with all our souls and with all our minds; directing all our intentions to you and seeking your honor in all things; with all our strength devoting every power and faculty of mind and body to the service of your love and to no other end.

"May we also love our neighbors as ourselves, drawing them to love of you with all our power; delighting in the good of others as in our own, sharing in their troubles, and giving no offense to any."

Ibid., 34–35.

Week Two: Day One

"Give us today our daily bread, which is your beloved Son, Jesus Christ our Lord, in the remembrance, understanding, and reverence of

the love that he bore us, and for the things that he said, did, and endured for our sakes.

"*Forgive us our sins* through your infinite mercy and by virtue of the passion of your beloved Son, our Lord Jesus Christ, and through the merits and prayers of the most blessed Virgin Mary and of all your elect."

Ibid., 35.

Week Two: Day Two

"*As we forgive those who sin against us,* and since we do not forgive fully, Lord, enable us to forgive fully so that we may truly love our enemies for your sake and pray for them devoutly to you, not returning evil for evil but seeking to serve all people in you.

Save us from the time of trial, hidden or open, sudden or persistent.

And deliver us from evil, past, present, and to come. Amen.

Ibid.

Week Two: Day Three

In the late fourth and early fifth centuries, John Cassian emerged as the leading figure in the burgeoning monastic movement. Before his death, he had either started or advanced the life of communities in Judaea, Egypt, Italy, and France. In his book, Conferences, he records the teaching of Abba Simon, who like most teachers of the time found the heights of prayer summarized in the Lord's Prayer.

"When we confess with our own mouths that the God and Lord of the universe is our Father, we claim that we have been called from our condition as slaves to adoption as children."

Keith Beasley-Topliffe, ed., *Making Life a Prayer: Selected Writings of John Cassian*, Upper Room Spiritual Classics 1 (Nashville, TN: Upper Room Books, 1997), 50.

Week Two: Day Four

Cassian continues to record Abba Simon's conference, which moves to the phrase "in heaven."

"We add next *in heaven*, so that, by shunning with the utmost horror all lingering in this present life, which we pass upon this earth as a pilgrimage, . . . we may instead hurry with all eagerness to that country where we confess that our Father dwells. May we not allow anything . . . to deprive us as a disgrace to our Father's inheritance and so make us incur the wrath of God's justice and severity."

Ibid., 50–51.

Week Two: Day Five

We follow Abba Simon one more day through Cassian's writing, as he expounds on the next phrase: "hallowed be your name."

"When we testify that our desire and our joy are God's glory, we become imitators of Christ, who said, '*Those who speak on their own seek their own glory; but the one who seeks the glory of him who sent him is true, and there is nothing false in him.*' And so when we say to God, '*Hallowed be your name,'* we say in other words, . . . 'that you may be seen to be hallowed in our spiritual conduct.' This is fulfilled in our case when people see our *good works and give glory to our Father in heaven.*"

Cassian's *Conference 9* continues the phrase-by-phrase exposition of the Lord's Prayer given by Abba Simon. But we will turn to other saints for further comments.

Ibid., 51.

Week Two: Day Six

Julian of Norwich was one of God's lights in the fourteenth century. Very little is known of her life, but her writing, A Book of Showings, is a central text in the Christian mystical tradition. In the fourteenth revelation (chapters 43 and 44), she writes about a union of our will with God's will in a way that sheds light on the next phrase of the Lord's Prayer, "your will be done."

"Prayer is a witness that the soul wills as God wills. . . . God regards us with love and wants to make us sharers of God's good will and deeds. Therefore God stirs us to pray that we may do what delights God. For this prayer and good will (that we have as God's gift), God will reward us endlessly."

Keith Beasley-Topliffe, ed., *Encounter with God's Love: Selected Writings of Julian of Norwich*, Upper Room Spiritual Classics 2 (Nashville, TN: Upper Room Books, 1998), 41.

Week Two: Day Seven

Julian also offers good counsel about prayer that reflects the next phrase in the Lord's Prayer, "on earth as it is in heaven."

"Truth sees God, and wisdom beholds God, and from these two comes the third, and that is a marvelous delight in God, which is love. Where truth and wisdom are, truly there is love, coming from both of them. All are of God's making. . . . The human soul is a creature in which God has created the same properties. More and more it does what it was made for: it sees God and beholds God and loves God. So God rejoices in the creature and the creature in God, endlessly marveling."

Ibid., 43–44.

Week Three: Day One

At about the same time Julian in England was experiencing God and writing about it, Thomas à Kempis was doing similarly in Germany. We cannot fail to note insights into prayer from his work, The Imitation of Christ, *thought for a long time to be the best-read Christian writing other than the Bible. His words about the inner life further reinforce the motive of the Lord's Prayer—doing God's will here and now on earth—in even the smallest and simplest of things.*

"If your heart is free from ill-ordered affection, no good deed will be difficult for you. If you aim at and seek after nothing but the pleasure of God and the welfare of your neighbor, you will enjoy freedom within.

"If your heart were right, then every created thing would be a mirror of life for you and a book of holy teaching. There is no creature so small and worthless that it does not show forth the goodness of God."

Keith Beasley-Topliffe, ed., *A Pattern for Life: Selected Writings of Thomas à Kempis*, Upper Room Spiritual Classics 2 (Nashville, TN: Upper Room Books, 1998), 27.

Week Three: Day Two

We must not think that doing God's will is achievable through mere human effort or ingenuity. The exercise of our wills is made possible by God's grace. Thomas makes this quite clear.

"When the grace of God comes to people, they can do all things, but when it leaves them, they become poor and weak, as if abandoned to affliction. Yet in this condition they should not become dejected or despair. On the contrary, they should calmly await the will of God and bear whatever befalls them in praise of Jesus

Christ, for after winter comes summer, after night, the day, and after the storm, a great calm."

Ibid., 33.

Week Three: Day Three

We travel to Spain where Teresa of Ávila ministered and wrote in the sixteenth century. In her book The Way of Perfection, *Teresa writes specifically about the Lord's Prayer. Her comments will complete our look at it. We begin with "give us this day our daily bread"; for Teresa, this aspect centered on receiving Holy Communion daily.*

"In no matter how many ways the soul may desire to eat, it will find delight and consolation in the most Blessed Sacrament. There is no need or trial or persecution that is not easy to suffer if we begin to enjoy the delight and consolation of this sacred bread.

" . . . Be with [Jesus] willingly; don't lose so good an occasion for conversing with Him as is the hour after having received Communion."

Teresa goes on to teach that from this means of grace, the rest of our lives will be made holy bread as we recognize the life-giving presence of Christ each day.

Keith Beasley-Topliffe, ed., *The Soul's Passion for God: Selected Writings of Teresa of Ávila*, Upper Room Spiritual Classics 1 (Nashville, TN: Upper Room Books, 1997); 39, 41.

Week Three: Day Four

Teresa goes on to speak to her companion Sisters about the next phrase in the Lord's Prayer, "forgive us our debts, as we forgive our debtors."

"This is a matter . . . that we should reflect upon very much: that something so serious and important, as that our Lord forgive us our faults, which deserve eternal fire, be done by means of something so lowly as our forgiving others. . . .

"Well, consider carefully that [Jesus] says, 'as we forgive,' as though it were something already being done. . . .

"I cannot believe that a person who comes so close to Mercy itself, where he realizes what he is and the great deal God has pardoned him of, would fail to pardon his offender immediately, in complete ease, and with a readiness to remain on very good terms with him."

Ibid., 43–47.

Week Three: Day Five

Teresa uses the phrase "lead us not into temptation" to speak about the temptations that come to those who pray. She warns about feelings of unworthiness on the one hand and self-assurance on the other.

"Thus, Eternal Father, what can we do but have recourse to You and pray that these enemies of ours not lead us into temptation? Let public enemies come, for by Your favor we will be more easily freed. But these other [more subtle] treacheries; who will understand them, my God? We always need to pray to You for a remedy. Instruct us, Lord, so that we may understand ourselves and be secure."

Ibid., 50.

Week Three: Day Six

We bring our brief examination of the Lord's Prayer to an end, but we stay with Teresa one more day as she reminds us that there is no one-size-fits-all pattern or program in prayer.

"It is important to understand that God doesn't lead all by one path, and perhaps the one who thinks she is walking along a very lowly path is in fact higher in the eyes of the Lord. . . .

". . . Let them consider how true humility consists very much in great readiness to be content with whatever the Lord may want to do with them and in always finding oneself unworthy to be called His servant."

Ibid., 31, 33.

Week Three: Day Seven

For the remainder of our thirty-one-day "school of prayer," we will let other saints instruct us in various ways about the life of prayer. We begin with an early desert mother, Amma Sarah, who rightly made purity of heart the center of prayer.

"If I prayed God that all people should approve of my conduct, I should find myself a penitent at the door of each one, but I shall rather pray that my heart may be pure toward all."

Beasley-Topliffe, *Seeking a Purer Christian Life*, 58.

Week Four: Day One

One more teacher from early Christianity, Abba Zeno, puts the needed note of realism into prayer, reminding us that we do not fully pray until we pray for our enemies.

"If a man wants God to hear his prayer quickly, then before he prays for anything else, even his own soul, when he stands and stretches out his hands toward God, he must pray with all his heart for his enemies. Through this action God will hear everything that he asks."

Ibid., 60.

Week Four: Day Two

In the latter half of the fourteenth century, Catherine of Siena came to the fore in Italy as a spiritual guide and a person deeply involved in matters of church and state. Her life was clearly founded upon and fueled by prayer as expressed in the following words of a letter sent to a group of women in Naples:

"Where shall we sense the fragrance of obedience, if not in prayer? Where strip ourselves of the self-love that makes us impatient when insulted or made to suffer? Or put on a divine love that will make us patient, and ready to glory in the cross of Christ crucified? In prayer."

Keith Beasley-Topliffe, ed., *A Life of Total Prayer: Selected Writings of Catherine of Siena*, Upper Room Spiritual Classics 3 (Nashville, TN: Upper Room Books, 2000), 34.

Week Four: Day Three

In the latter half of the sixteenth century, Saint John of the Cross arose in Spain, taking friends and followers into a deep understanding of the spiritual life. In the book The Dark Night of the Soul *John records how prayer is embedded and expressed from start to finish in the soul's journey.*

"God nurtures and caresses the soul, after it has been resolutely converted to his service, like a loving mother who warms her child with the heat of her bosom, nurses it with good milk and tender food, and carries and caresses it in her arms. . . .

"The soul finds its joy, therefore, in spending lengthy periods at prayer."

Keith Beasley-Topliffe, ed., *Loving God through the Darkness: Selected Writings of John of the Cross*, Upper Room Spiritual Classics 3 (Nashville, TN: Upper Room Books, 2000), 43.

Week Four: Day Four

Saint John knows that a deeper spiritual life and a richer life of prayer move beyond simple response to God's blessings. At some time the soul lives unto God without prior stimulation. This difficult kind of praying signals maturity in the spiritual life.

"Many spiritual persons, after having exercised themselves in approaching God through images, forms, and meditations suitable for beginners, err greatly if they do not determine, dare, or know how to detach themselves from these palpable methods to which they are accustomed. For God then wishes to lead them to more . . . invisible graces by removing the gratification. . . .

"The proper advice for these individuals is that they must learn to abide in that quietude with a loving attentiveness to God."

Ibid., 39, 41.

Week Four: Day Five

In the eighteenth century, William Law arose as an influential spiritual guide for many people. Christians today still read his book A Serious Call to a Devout and Holy Life. *He urges us to remember that deep prayer is not reserved for a select few; it is for ordinary people in any walk of life.*

"Prayer is a duty that belongs to all states and conditions of people. . . .

". . . [All Christians] make it a rule to be content and thankful in every part and accident of life, because it comes from God. . . .

"Unless the common course of our lives is according to the common spirit of our prayers, our prayers are so far from being a real or sufficient degree of devotion that they become an empty lip service or, what is worse, a notorious hypocrisy."

Keith Beasley-Topliffe, ed., *Total Devotion to God: Selected Writings of William Law*, Upper Room Spiritual Classics 3 (Nashville, TN: Upper Room Books, 2000), 43.

Week Four: Day Six

In 1926 Evelyn Underhill published a book titled Concerning the Inner Life. *The origin of its content was a retreat talk she had given to instruct parish clergy. In it, she established prayer as the primary act not only of the priesthood but of all Christians.*

"Take first then, as primary, the achievement and maintenance of a right attitude toward God; that profound and awestruck sense of God's transcendent reality, that humbly adoring relation, on which all else depends. I feel no doubt that, for all who take the spiritual life seriously, this prayer of adoration exceeds all other types in educational and purifying power."

Keith Beasley-Topliffe, ed., *The Soul's Delight: Selected Writings of Evelyn Underhill*, Upper Room Spiritual Classics 2 (Nashville, TN: Upper Room Books, 1998), 14.

Week Four: Day Seven

We bring our school of prayer to a close by reading the words of one of Japan's best-known Christian saints: Toyohiko Kagawa. From the early years of the twentieth century until his death in 1960, Kagawa labored in ministries of evangelism and social reform. His life of prayer undergirded it all. His words inspire us to make prayer our primary "work," from which all our other works arise and flow.

"Prayer is not merely petition, but is coming face-to-face with God . . . it is . . . not necessary to use difficult classical expressions. If we just talk as we would to our human father, it is enough. For a little child to say, 'Thank you, God. Amen,' is all right."

Keith Beasley-Topliffe, ed., *Living Out Christ's Love: Selected Writings from Toyohiko Kagawa*, Upper Room Spiritual Classics 2 (Nashville, TN: Upper Room Books, 1998), 35.

A RULE OF LIFE

THE HISTORY OF CHRISTIAN spirituality reveals that our formation into Christ is not a random or haphazard enterprise. Saints of the ages have developed orders of devotion to provide specificity, guidance, and maturation. One term for such an order is *a rule of life*.

The word *rule* does not mean a law to be kept (with punishment for failure) but rather living a life that is "regulated" (directed) toward desired ends. Some of those ends are ongoing (for example, practicing the spiritual disciplines and means of grace); others can be set for prescribed periods of time (for example, the next six months). The ends can also be distributed into units (for example, daily, weekly, monthly, quarterly, semiannually). They also relate to all aspects of life (for example, personal, marital, family, friends, work, play, diet, exercise, sleep, and rest). They can shape us inwardly, motivate us outwardly, and relate us collectively.

A rule of life can result in a personalized guide for growth that connects classical practices of the ages with real-life goals and needs at a particular point of our journey. This guide to prayer is written with the hope that you will use it in the context of a larger rule of life that you create for yourself and amend from time to time. Daily prayer is only one part of a devotional life.

The following template gives you an opportunity to construct a simple rule of life. Using the next three months as your time line, consider what attitudes and actions you would cultivate in relation to the following categories:

Daily

Weekly

Monthly

Quarterly

The Christian's Holy Habits

In *A Pocket Prayer Book* Ralph Cushman wrote a limited Rule of Life, which follows. It is not as broad as you may want yours to be, but its classic beauty is exemplary.

I believe in habits: I believe habits make or break us: I believe habits send us to heaven or hell. Therefore I believe in HOLY habits.

Indeed, so sure am I that a happy Christian life depends upon some four or five habits that if some person should come to me and say, "Prescribe what I must do to have glad fellowship with Jesus Christ, here and hereafter," I would say:

First. Form the habit of keeping holy some portion of each day for Bible reading and prayer. Make this your first business.

Second. Form the habit of giving every week a definite proportion of your time in special service to your fellow men [and women], in the name of Christ and of His church.

Third. Make attendance at public worship the fixed habit of your life. Allow yourself no excuse for nonattendance that you would not give to your associates in business.

Fourth. Form the habit of accepting every opportunity to receive the Sacrament of the Lord's Supper. Christ will meet you in the Communion. Jesus says, "I am the bread of life."

Fifth. Form the holy habit of setting apart a definite proportion of your money for the work of the Kingdom. Make it the first draft upon your income; set it aside with prayer; use it carefully as unto God. Have faith to begin with "at least a tenth." This habit will be for you a trusty ther-mometer, marking the temper of your life.

These, my friends, are the holy habits I recom-mend. Others will follow on. Behind them all, of course, must be the hunger after God: but with these habits formed, you have the certain helps that God has sent to bless your days; and more than this, to make you a faithful steward of the Church of Christ.

—R. S. C.

Lectio Divina

LECTIO DIVINA is a way of praying, often referred to as "sacred reading." In prayer we respond to God's initiative. In *lectio*, we respond to God in relation to a text that we are pondering. *Lectio* has been practiced since at least the fourth century AD as a means of grace to engage the mind, heart, emotions, and will.

The goal of *lectio* is conformity to the way of Christ by allowing the risen Christ to abide in us and us in him. In this formative reading we ask God to give us a word that we may live and, in turn, be life-givers to others.

In the following pages, I provide a brief summary of each dimension of *lectio divina*. Do not think of them as separate steps but more as interacting dynamics that enable the written Word to become the living Word in us and through us.

Pray

Prayer winds its way through the entirety of *lectio divina*. It is the "atmosphere" in which we practice *lectio divina*. But at specific points we pray in relation to particular things.

We begin our time of *lectio* in prayer, asking God to come to us in the Spirit to inspire, inform, and guide us as we read. As we read, we pause to pray as particular words and phrases catch our attention. We ask God to plant these words into our heart, so that they may bear fruit. At the end of our time of reading, we pray, asking God for the grace to apply the Word (message) to us in such a way that we may be doers of the Word and not hearers only.

Read

In *lectio* we read ultimately to be formed, not just informed. For some of us, this is a new way to read. We have been trained to read in order to gain facts, pass tests, etc. But in *lectio*, we read to draw near to God and allow God to draw near to us.

We begin our reading by settling down and quieting ourselves. Some days this takes longer than others, but it is part of the process. We remain unrushed, and we have no fixed amount of text to read. We read slowly, giving words and phrases time to engage us. We read systematically through a Bible book, encountering the text in its original flow.

We read with the intention of obeying, so we ask God to "give us a word that we may live." We do not force or control what that word becomes for us during a certain period of reading. We simply receive with gratitude what God gives us.

Meditate

Meditation means to ponder, to take the "word" we have been given in our reading and walk around it. Hugh of Saint Victor called it "piercing the core of a particular truth." We may sometimes use additional resources (for example, biblical languages, other texts, concordances, dictionaries, hymnals, poems, stories, previous life experiences) to further enrich the word we have been given. In meditation we are free to study the word, but we do so in a way that invites the word to "study" us. We do not attempt to master it; we ask the word to master us.

In meditation we must guard against becoming busy and distracted. We are called to continue to rest in God, but now with the leisure to explore the word we've been given— much like enjoying a focused conversation with a good friend. Evelyn Underhill called it "thinking in the presence of God."

Contemplate

Contemplation literally means being "with" (*con*) the "observations" (*templari*). The observations are the words (sentence, phrase, message) we've been given in our reading and pondered in our meditation. We now seek to become "one" (united) with the message, desiring the written word to become the living word in us.

As previously stated, we aim to be increasingly conformed to Christ—to allow his mind, heart, and work to inspire us. Life by Christ, with Christ, in Christ, and for Christ is our heart's desire. Contemplation is the dynamic in *lectio divina* where we abide in Christ and he abides in us. It is a mystery, just as the formation of any holy relationship can never be fully described. But we have been made in the image of God and that implies the capacity for relationship. Contemplation is the cultivating of our relationship with God, using the word we've been given as each day's focal point.

Act

This term was not originally separated from contemplation; but in recent times, it has been highlighted as a reminder that in *lectio divina* we not only *believe* the word, we *behave* it. Our heart desires that the word we've been given will become influential within us and through us.

Before we leave the time devoted to *lectio divina*, we prayerfully ask, "God, how might I put this word into practice for my good and your glory?" We need not ask for anything large or grand. Most often, the nudge will be toward something simple and practical. As Brother Lawrence, a seventeenth-century Carmelite monk, reminded us: "We can do little things for God."

In the action-dimension, we return throughout the day to the word we've been given, seeking to use it as a concrete means to fulfill the two great commandments: loving God and loving our neighbors as we love ourselves.

GROWING IN PRAYER

EVERY GUIDE TO PRAYER assumes growth in the life of prayer. We never "arrive." We are always building on the present. We are always beginners when exploring Mystery and the Infinite. The marks of the spiritual life are love (of God and neighbor) and humility (always relying on grace and hungering for more). We are always open and alert to resources that will help us grow in the mind, heart, and work of Christ.

Accordingly, I recommend the following resources. They barely scratch the surface in relation to what exists to assist us in our spiritual formation. But they offer some next steps to consider taking in your journey of faith. Some will directly guide you in your praying; others will place prayer in the larger context of the Christian spiritual life.

Beasley-Topliffe, Keith, ed., Upper Room Spiritual Classics (multiple volumes). Nashville, TN: Upper Room Books.

Classics of Western Spirituality series (multiple volumes). Mahwah, NJ: Paulist Press.

Dunnam, Maxie. *The Workbook on Abiding in Christ*. Nashville, TN: Upper Room Books, 2010.

_____. *The Workbook of Living Prayer*. Nashville, TN: Upper Room Books, 1994.

Foster, Richard J. *Celebration of Discipline: The Path to Spiritual Growth* (New York: HarperCollins Publishers, 2007).

_____. *Prayer: Finding the Heart's True Home* (San Francisco: HarperSanFrancisco, 1992).

HarperCollins Spiritual Classics (multiple volumes). New York: HarperCollins.

Harper, Steve. *Devotional Life in the Wesleyan Tradition: A Workbook*. Nashville, TN: Upper Room Books, 1995.

_____. *Talking in the Dark: Praying When Life Doesn't Make Sense*. Nashville, TN: Upper Room Books, 2007.

Job, Rueben P. and Norman Shawchuck. *A Guide to Prayer for All God's People*. Nashville, TN: Upper Room Books, 1990.

_____. *A Guide to Prayer for All Who Seek God*. Nashville, TN: Upper Room Books, 2006.

_____. *A Guide to Prayer for Ministers and Other Servants*. Nashville, TN: Upper Room Books, 1983.

Kidd, Sue Monk. *Firstlight: The Early Inspirational Writings of Sue Monk Kidd*. Nashville, TN: GuidepostsBooks, 2006.

Merton, Thomas. *Contemplative Prayer*. New York: Doubleday, 1989.

Mulholland Jr., M. Robert. *Invitation to a Journey: A Road Map for Spiritual Formation*. Downers Grove, IL: InterVarsity Press, 1993.

_____. *Shaped by the Word: The Power of Scripture in Spiritual Formation*, rev. ed. Nashville, TN: Upper Room Books, 2000.

Muto, Susan Annette. *Pathways of Spiritual Living*. Pittsburgh, PA: Epiphany Books, 2004.

Norris, Kathleen. *The Cloister Walk*. New York: Riverhead Books, 1997.

Nouwen, Henri J. M. *Making All Things New: An Invitation to the Spiritual Life*. San Francisco: HarperSanFrancisco, 1981.

Pennington, M. Basil *Lectio Divina: Renewing the Ancient Practice of Praying the Scriptures*. Spring Valley, NY: Crossroad Publishing, 1998.

The Book of Common Prayer. New York: Church Hymnal Corporation, 1979.

Underhill, Evelyn. *The Spiritual Life* (various publishers).

Vintage Spiritual Classics series (multivolume series). New York: Knopf Doubleday Publishing Group.

NOTE: more and more classical resources are becoming available online. One of the best sources is the Christian Classics Ethereal Library: www.ccel.org. Use your favorite search engine to look for specific people and titles.